Knights *through the* Ages

NAPOLEON, THE KINGS OF ITALY, AND AN EMPEROR

A TRAVEL PHOTO ART BOOK

LAINE CUNNINGHAM

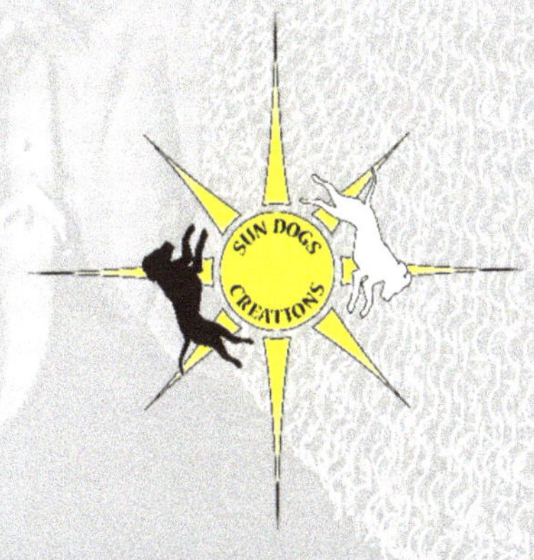

Knights Through the Ages

Napoleon, the Kings of Italy, and an Emperor

A Travel Photo Art Book

Published by Sun Dogs Creations
Changing the World One Book at a Time
Print ISBN: 9781946732637

Cover Design by Angel Leya

THE TRAVEL PHOTO ART SERIES

Bikes of Berlin

Necropolises of New Orleans I & II

Ruins of Rome I & II

Ancients of Assisi I & II

Panoramas of Portugal

Nuances of New York

Glimpses of Germany

Impressions of Italy

Coast of California

Altitudes of the Alps

Utopia of the Unicorn

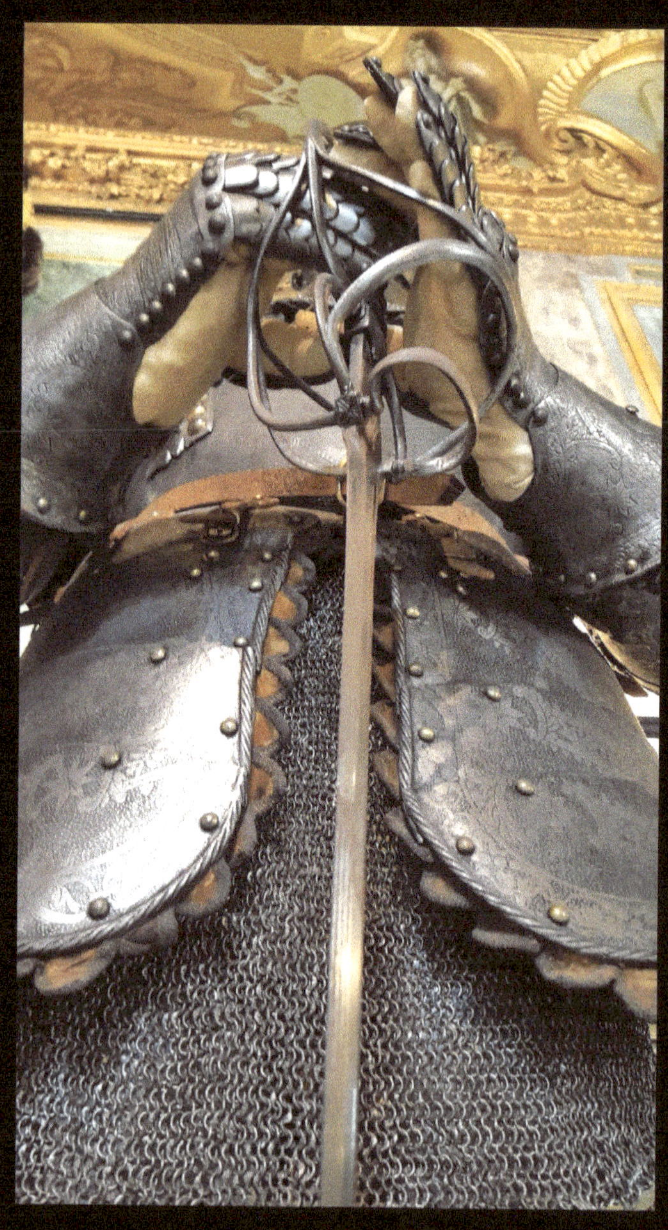

VESTMENT

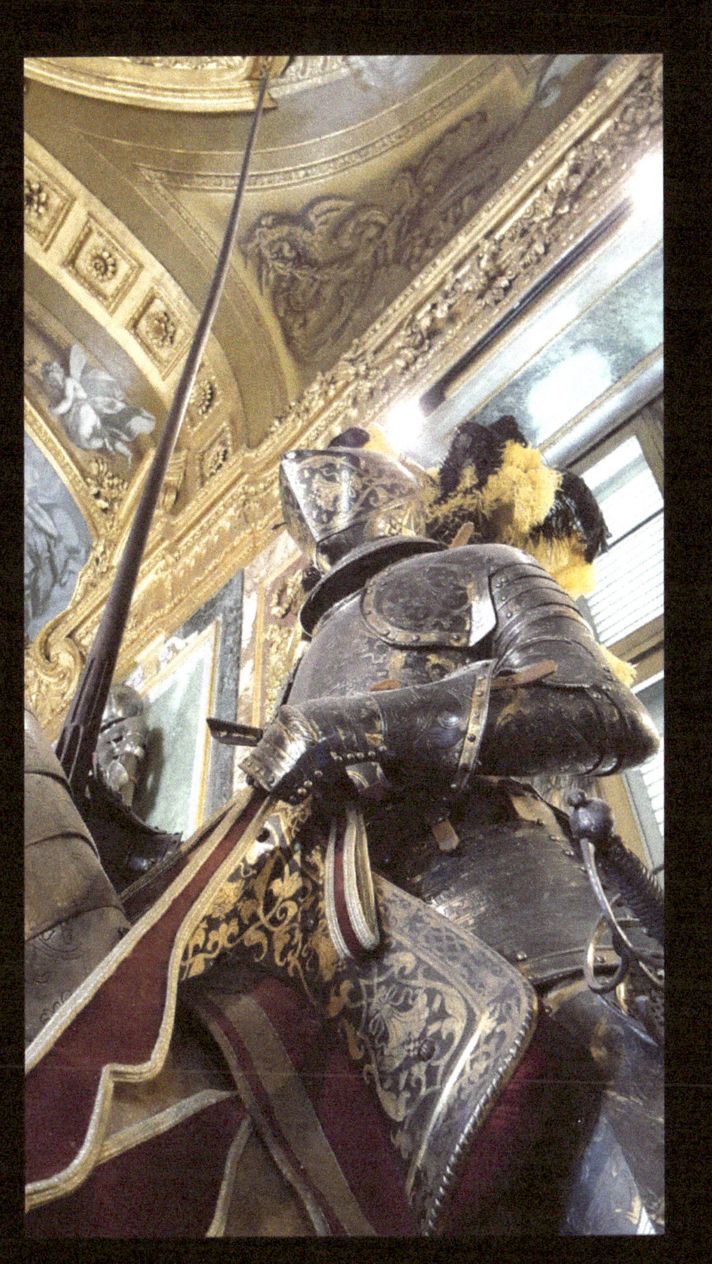

REGAL

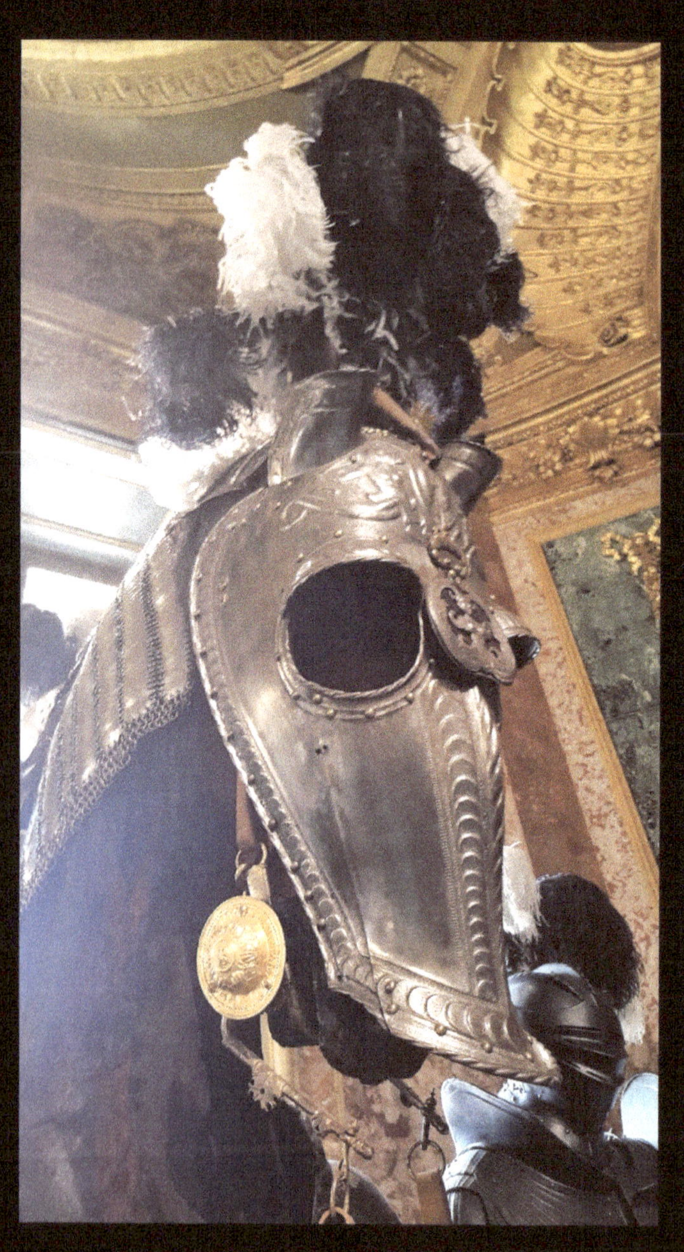

CHAMPING AT THE BIT

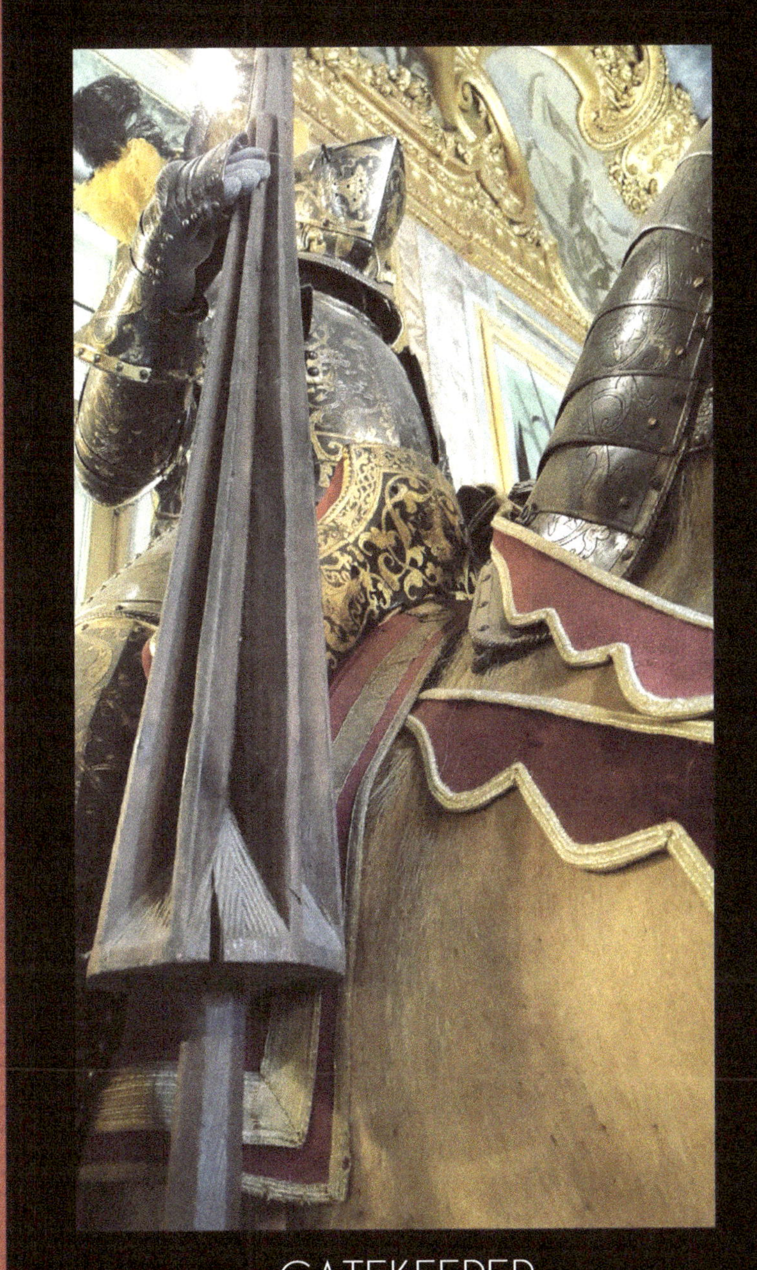

GATEKEEPER

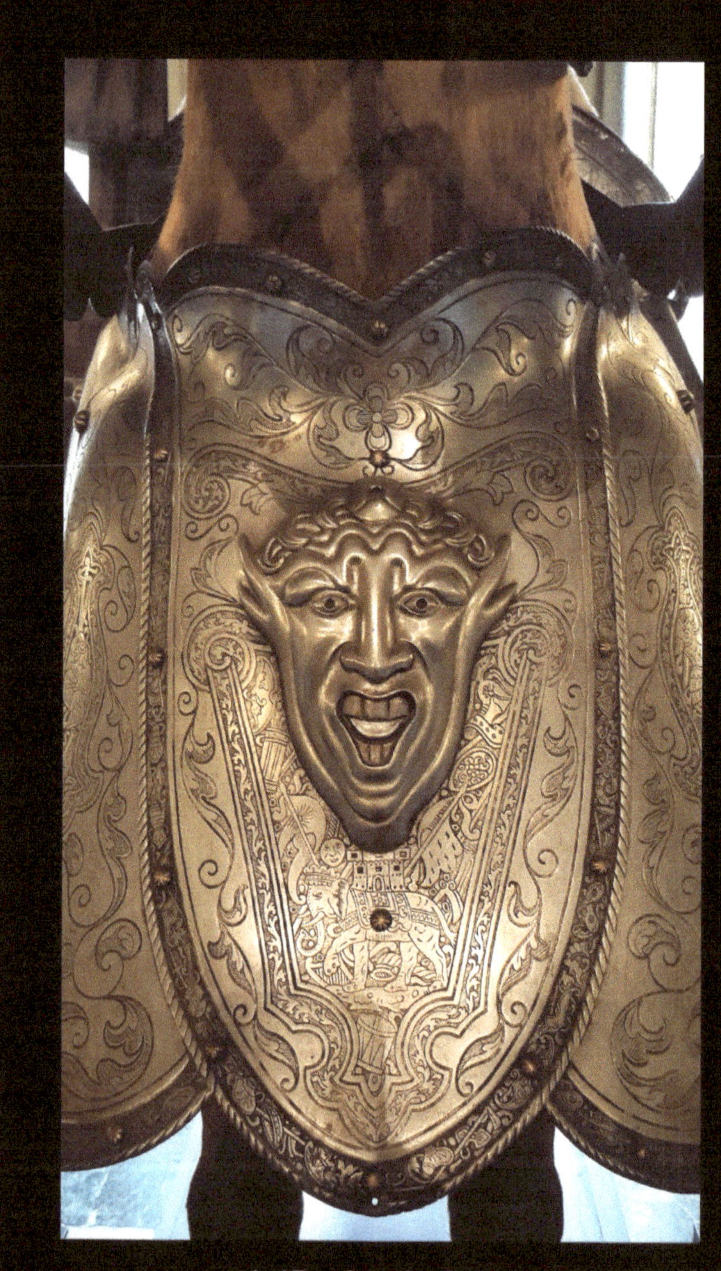

MR. SPOCK

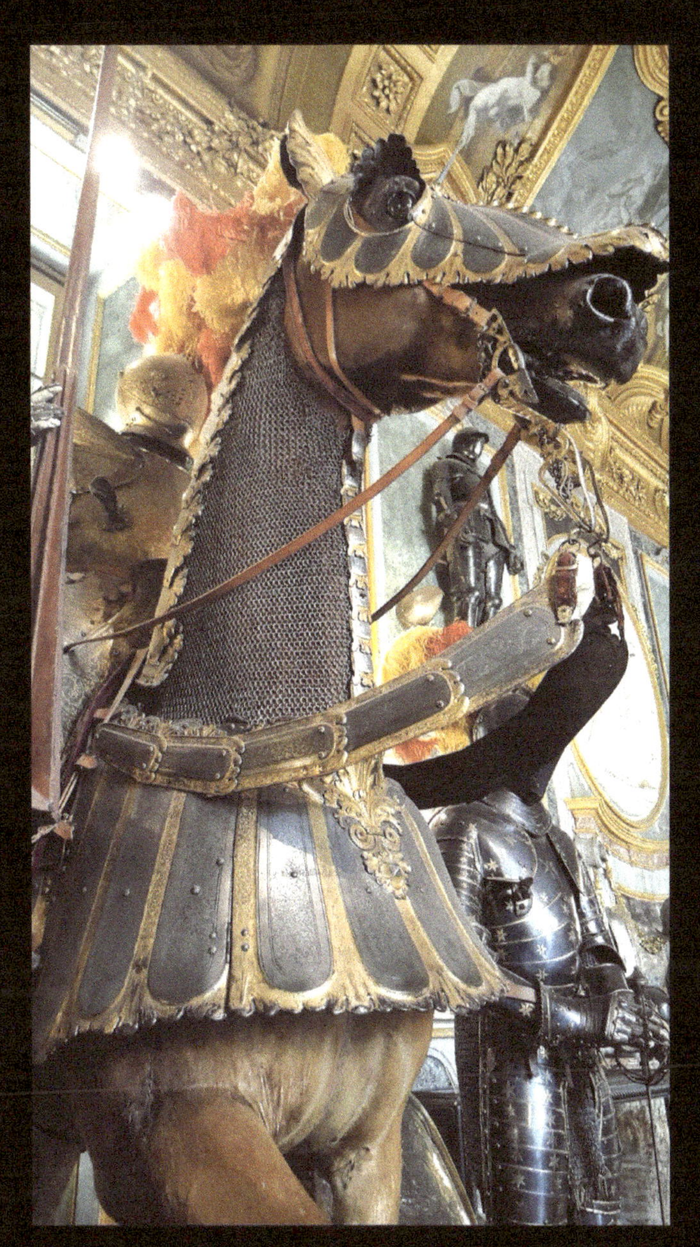

CAROUSEL

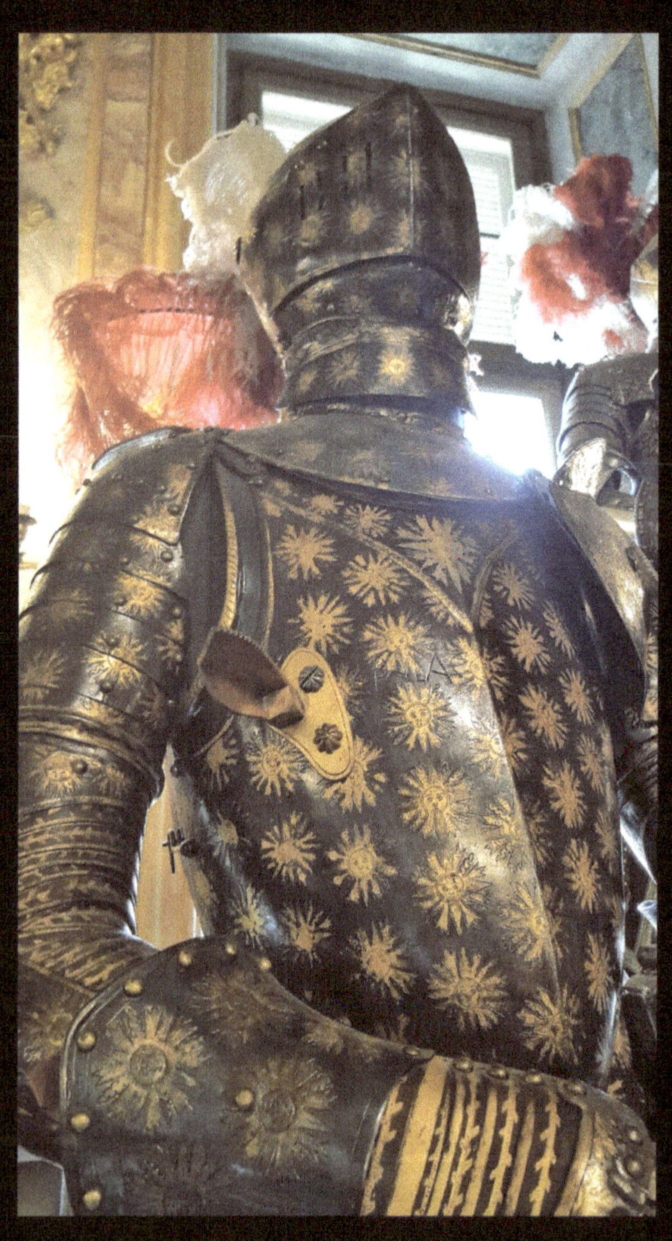

CLOSE-UP

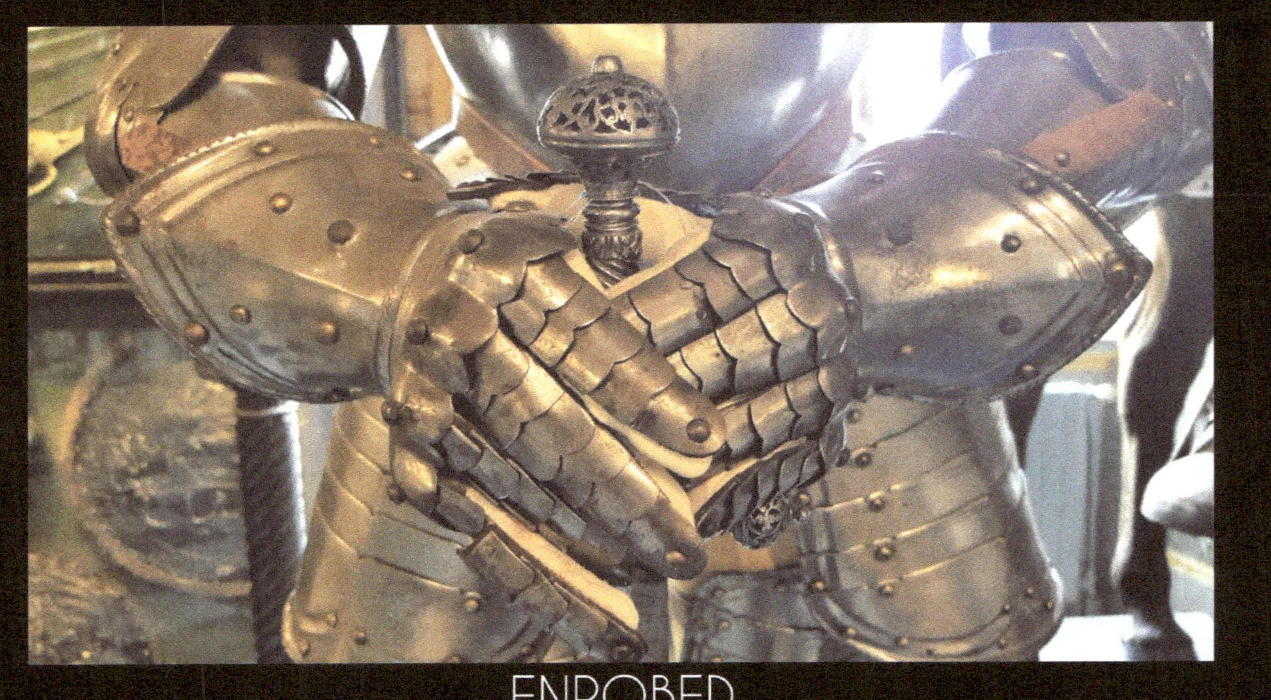

ENROBED

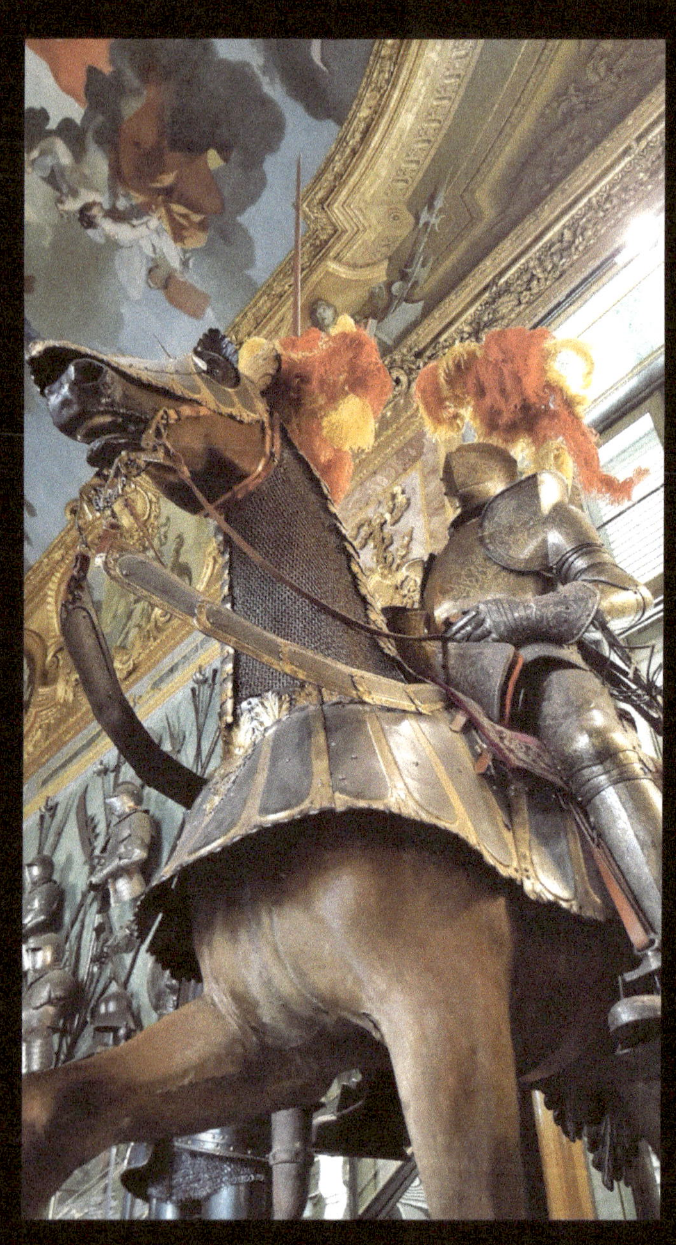

PRANCE

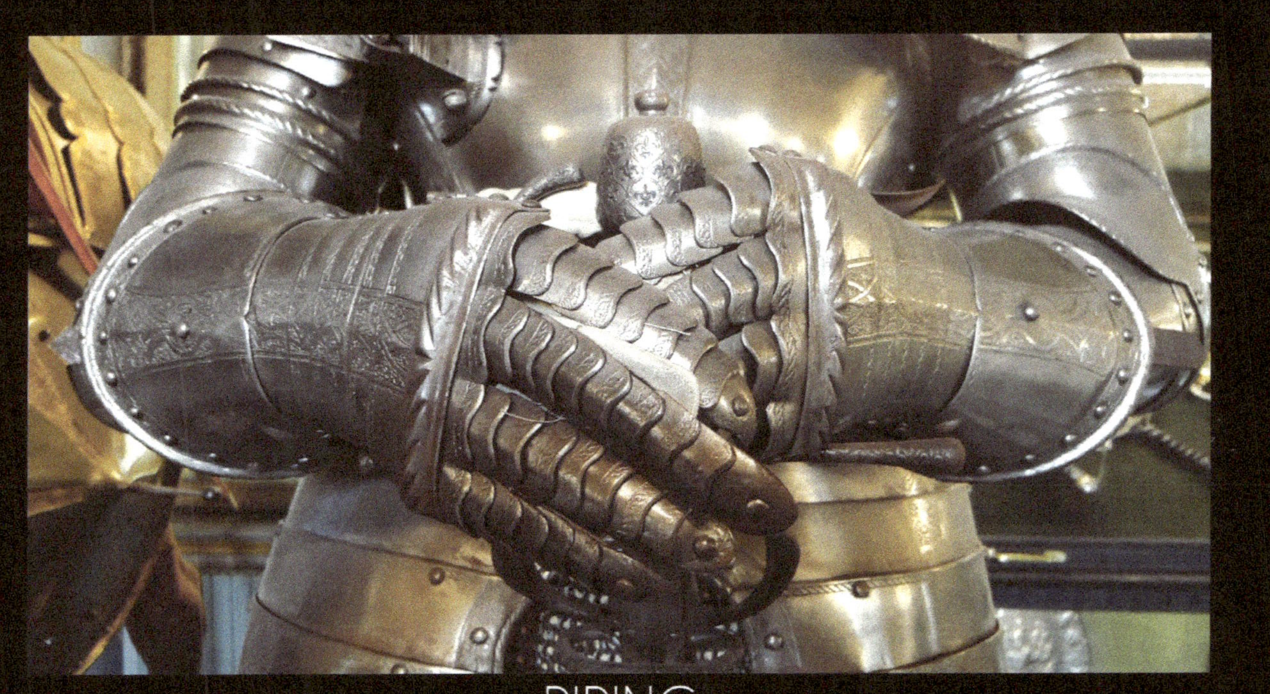

PIPING

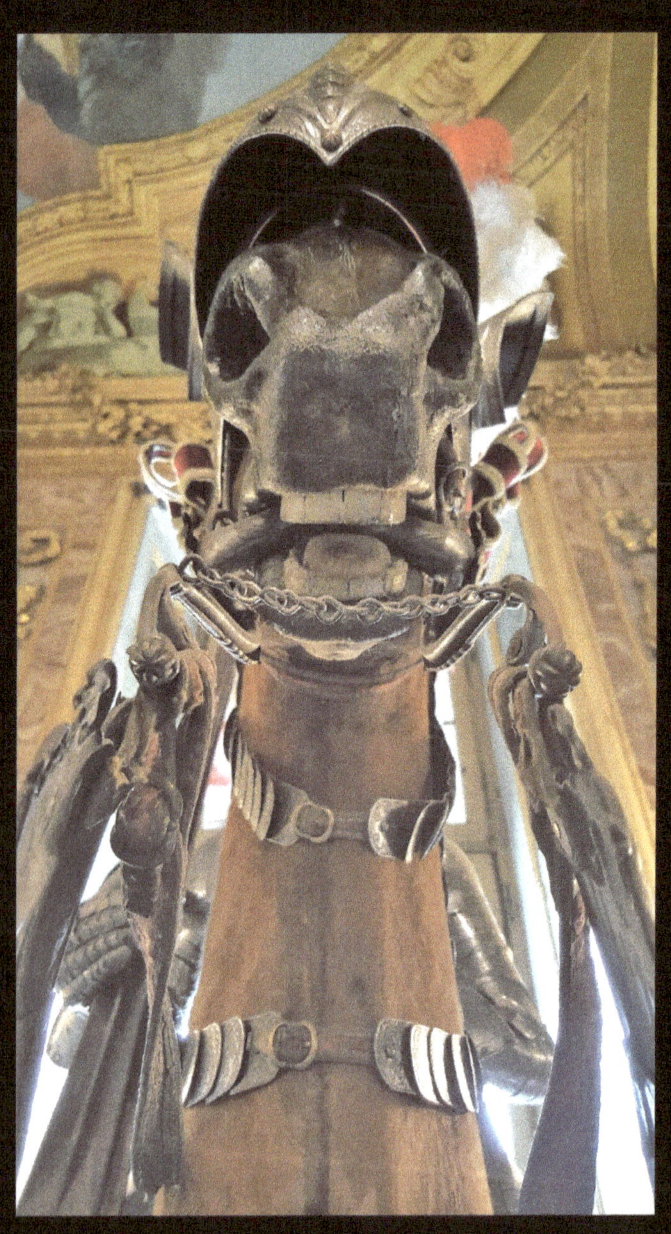

FROGMOUTH

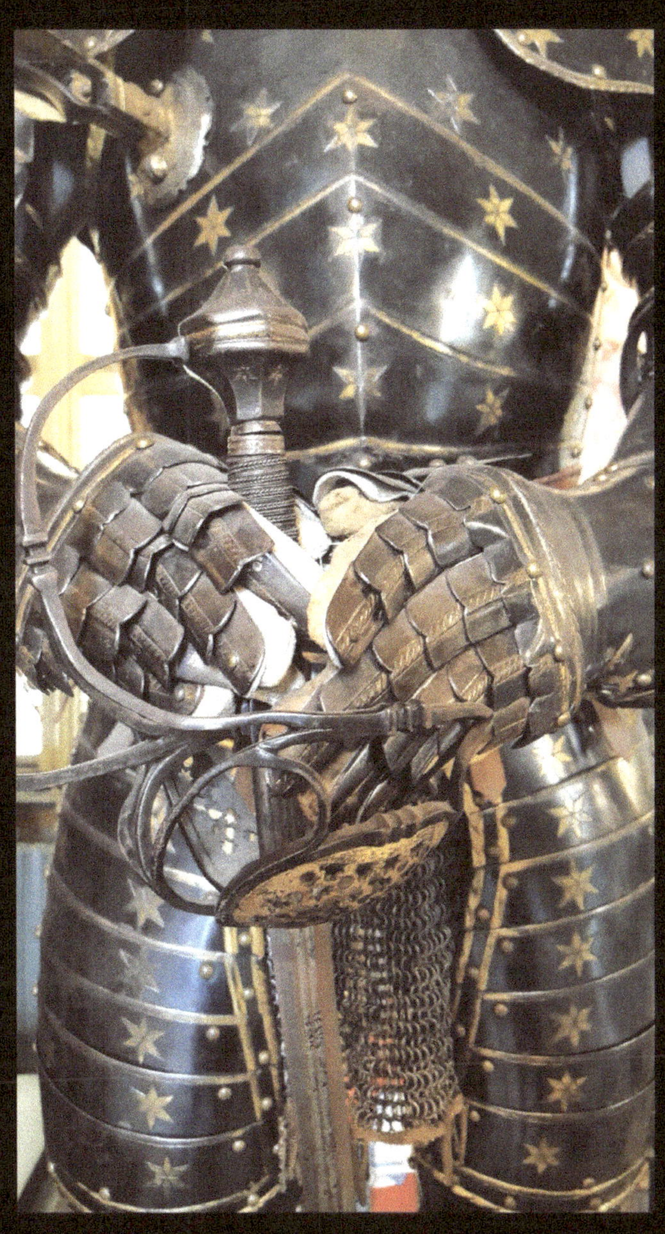

CRUSADER

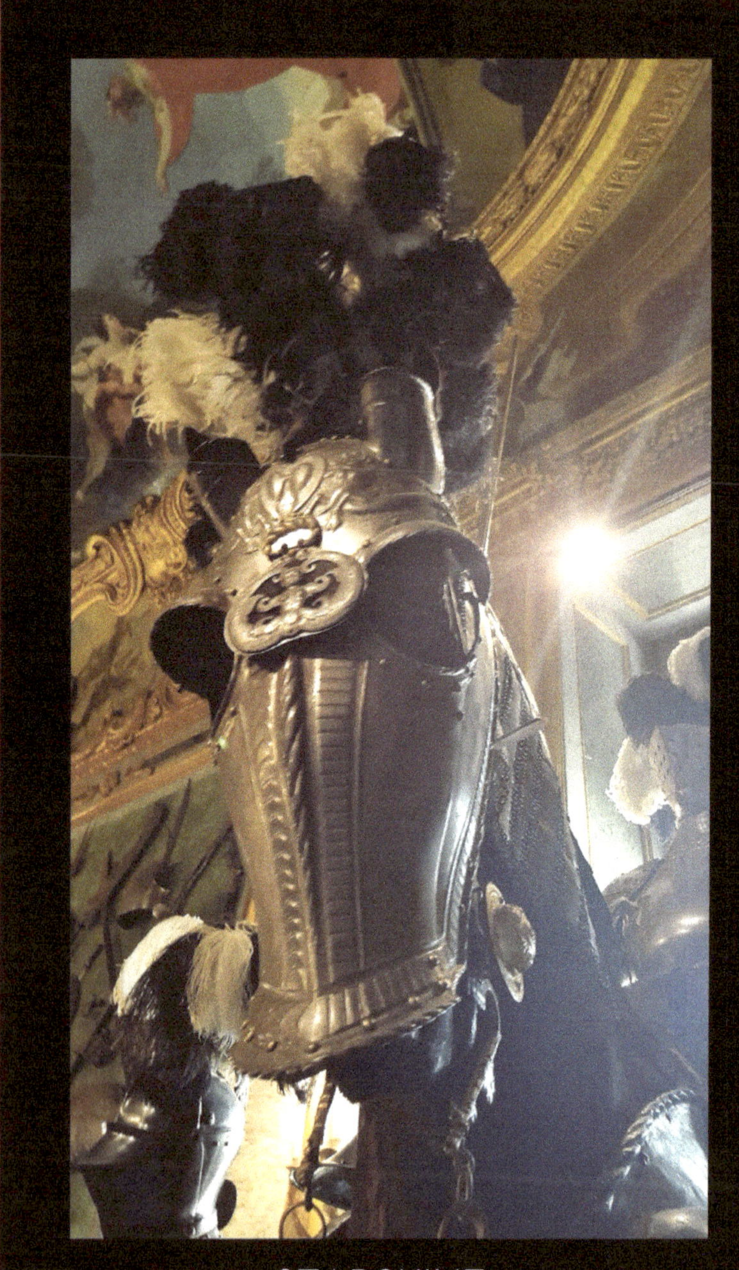

STARSHINE

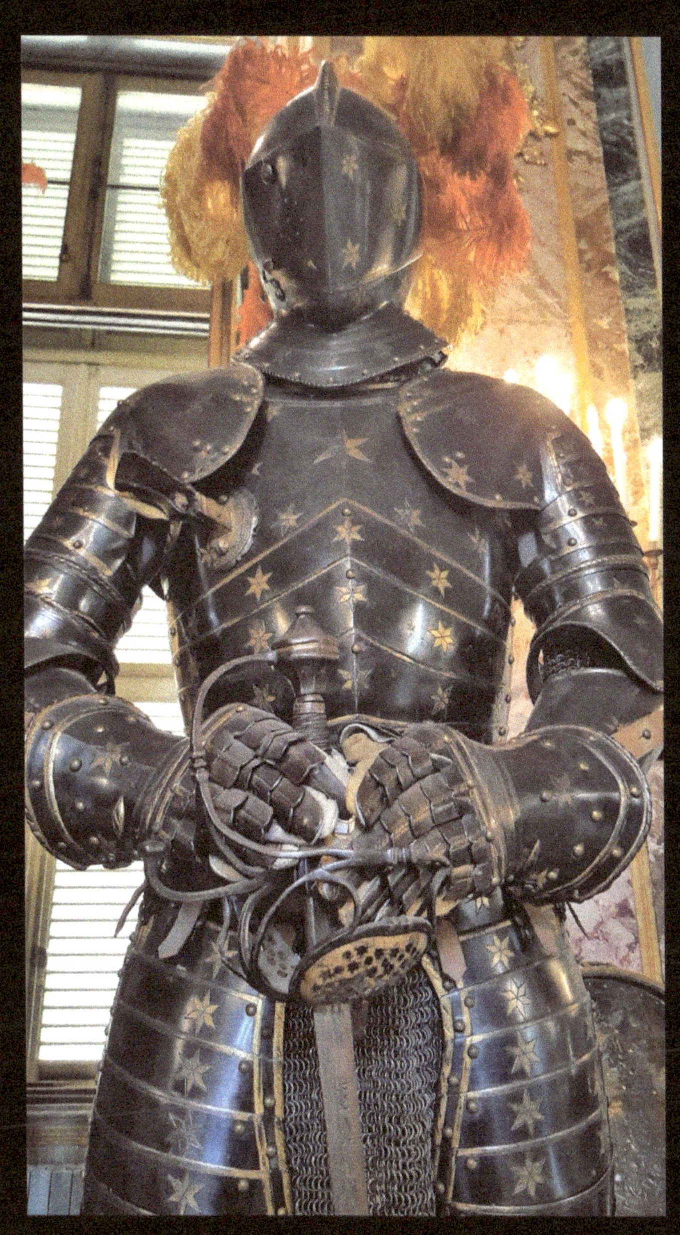

GENTLEMAN

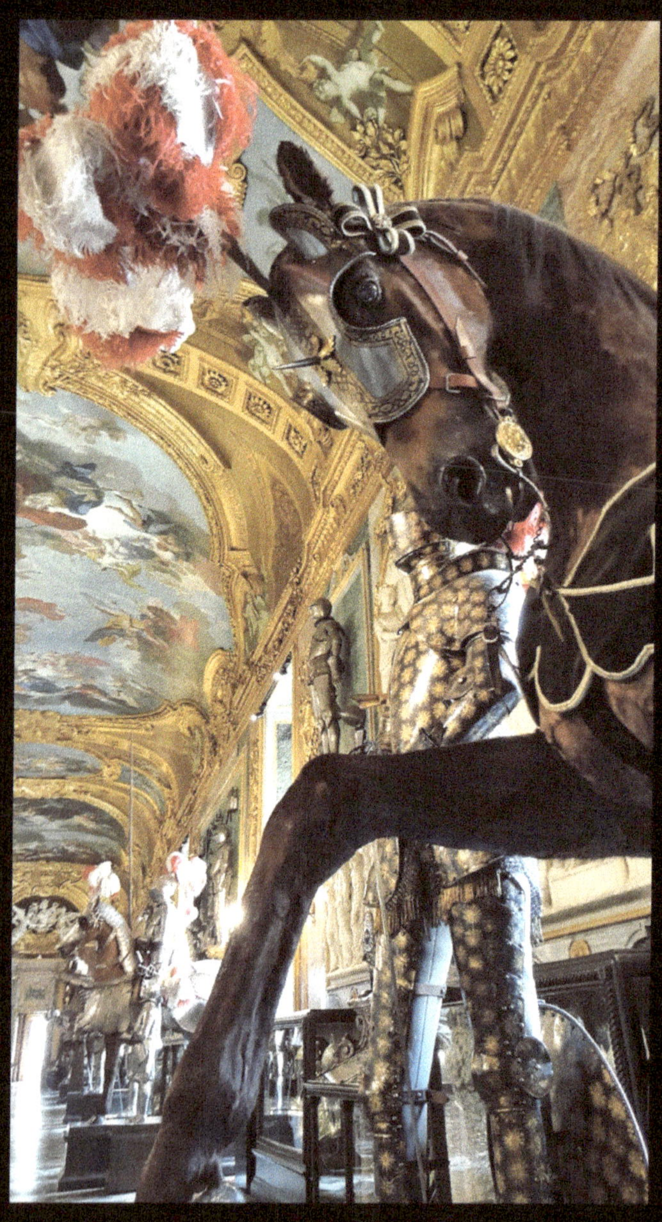

NICE TO MEET YOU

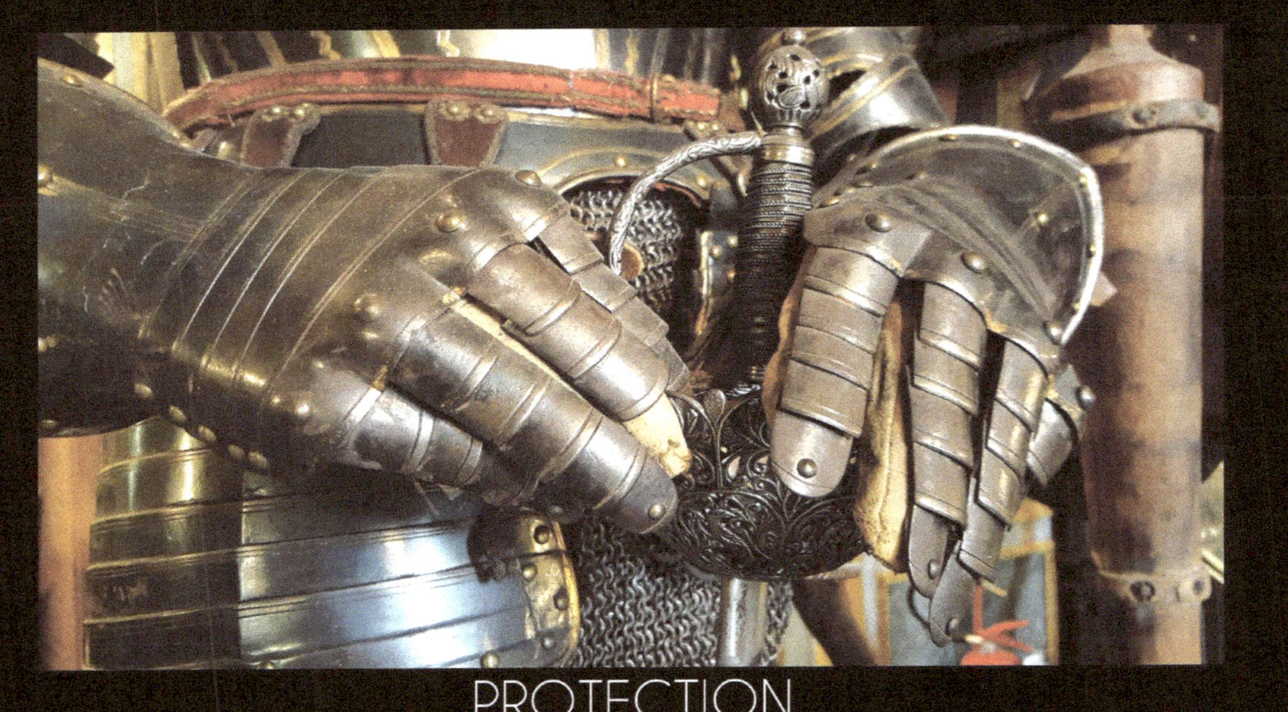
PROTECTION

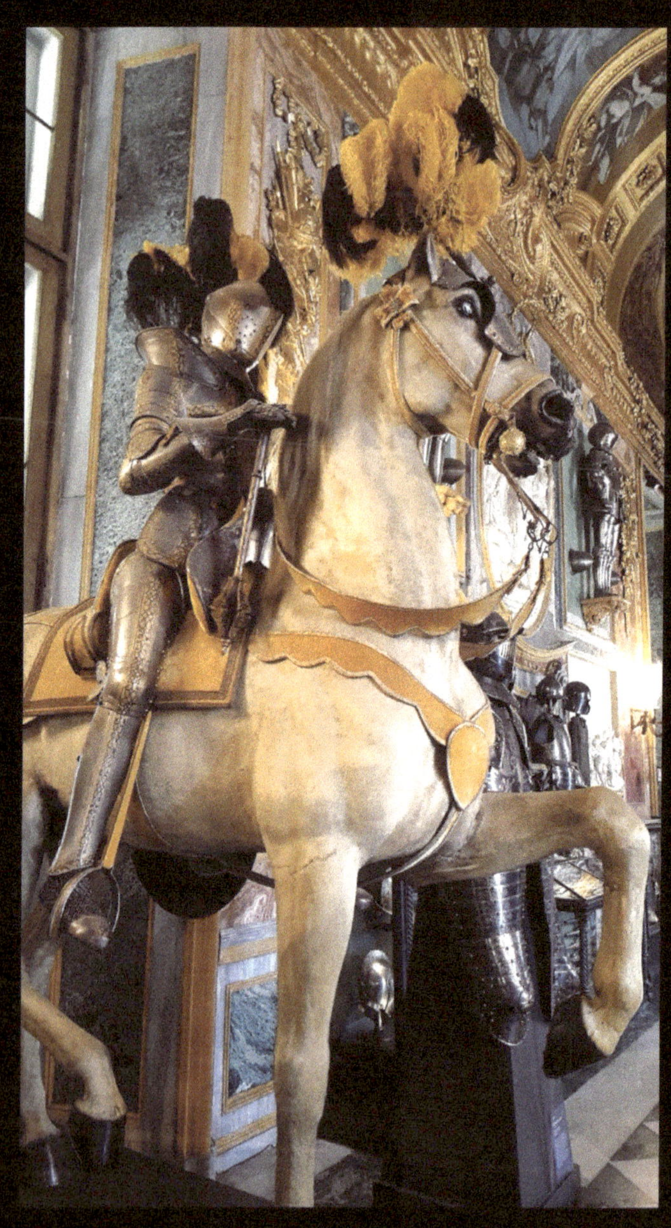

PONY BOY

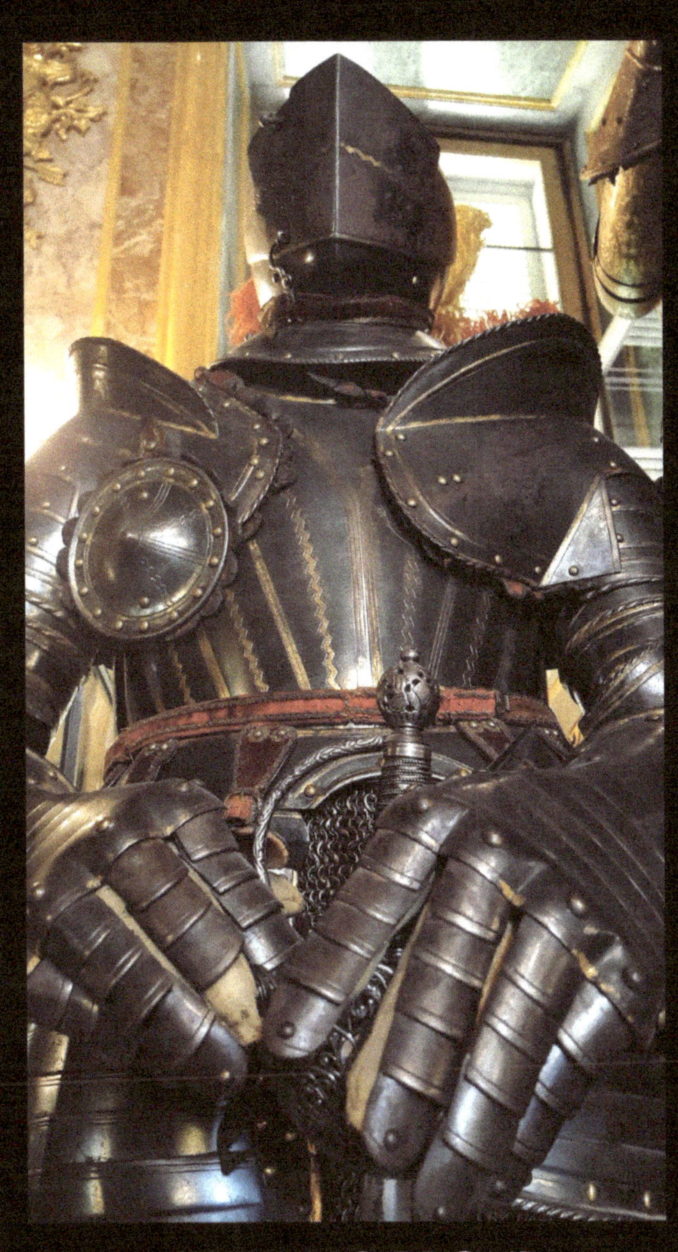

STANDING PROUD

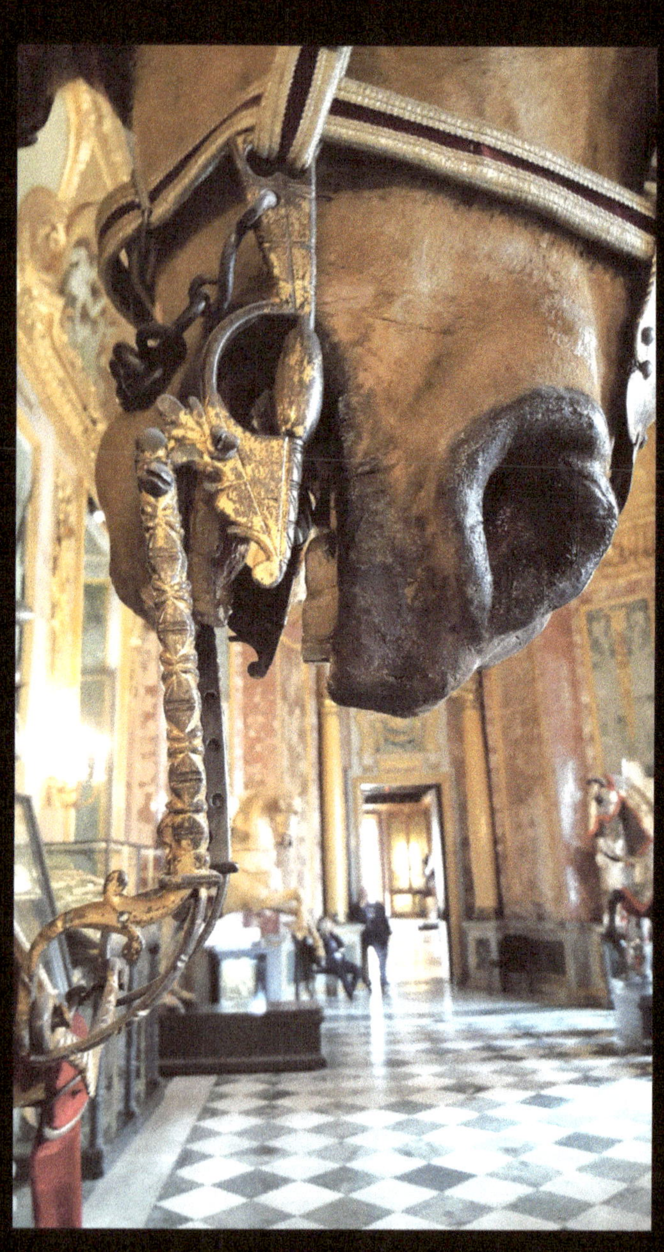

HANGING

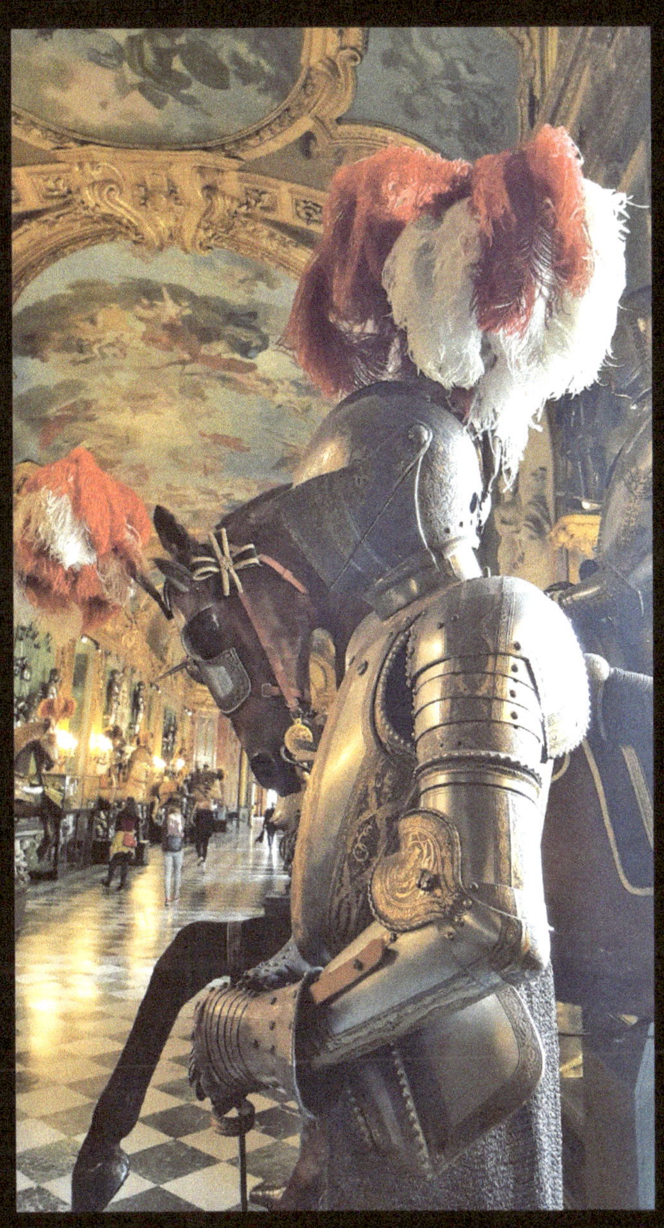

PARADE STANCE

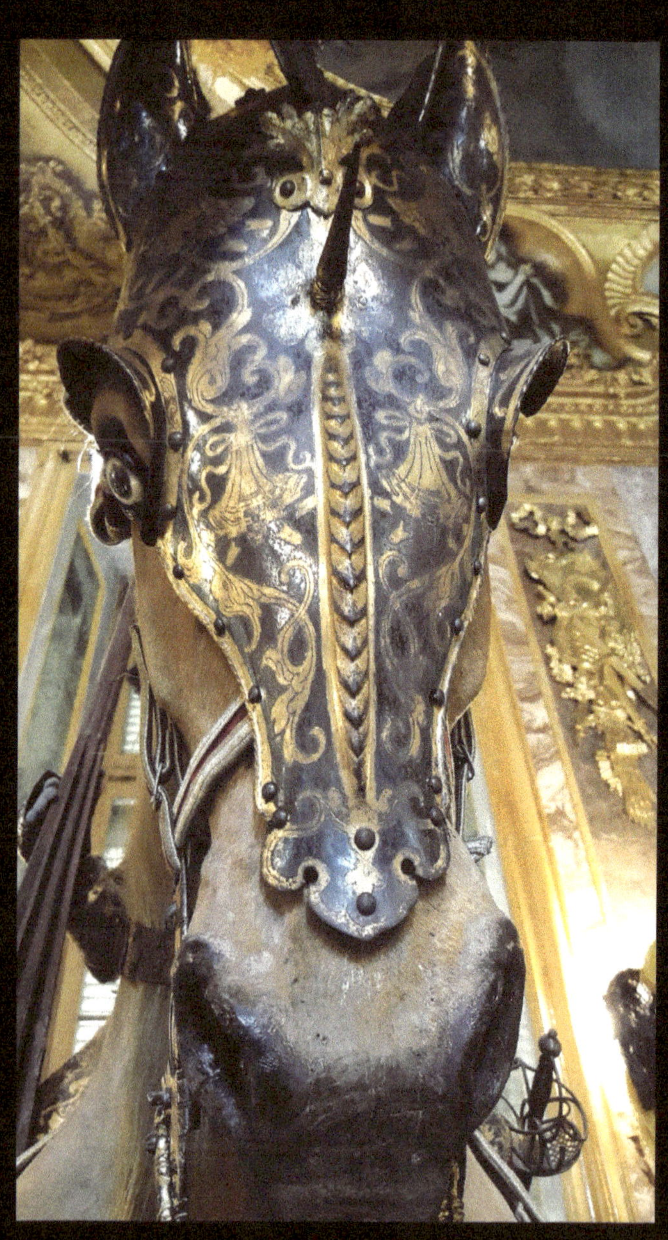

UNICORN

About the Author

Laine Cunningham is an award-winning novelist. Her women's travel adventure memoir *Woman Alone: A Six-Month Journey Through the Australian Outback* appeals to fans of *Wild* and *Eat Pray Love*.

Fiction

The Family Made of Dust

Beloved

Reparation

Nonfiction

Woman Alone

On the Wallaby Track: Australian Words and Phrases

Seven Sisters: Messages from Aboriginal Australia

Writing While Female or Black or Gay

The Zen of Travel
The Zen of Gardening
Zen in the Stable
The Zen of Chocolate
The Zen of Dogs

The Wisdom of Puppies
The Wisdom of Babies
The Wisdom of Weddings

Bikes of Berlin
Necropolises of New Orleans I & II
Ruins of Rome I & II
Ancients of Assisi I & II
Panoramas of Portugal
Nuances of New York
Glimpses of Germany
Impressions of Italy
Altitudes of the Alps
Coast of California
Knights Through the Ages
Utopia of the Unicorn

www.ingramcontent.com/pod-product-compliance
Ingram Content Group UK Ltd.
Pitfield, Milton Keynes, MK11 3LW, UK
UKHW062254290726
14090UKWH00017B/687